SCHOLASTIC

Let's Find Out

My REBUS Reader

Pumpkin Parts!

by Robert O'Toole

SCHOLASTIC INC.

New York Toronto London Auckland Sydney New Delhi Hong Kong

A  has a stem.

pumpkin

What colors are the shells of these pumpkins?

A  has a shell.

pumpkin

A  has pulp. Slimy!

pumpkin

A  has seeds.

pumpkin

A  has flesh.

pumpkin

This  has a face!

pumpkin

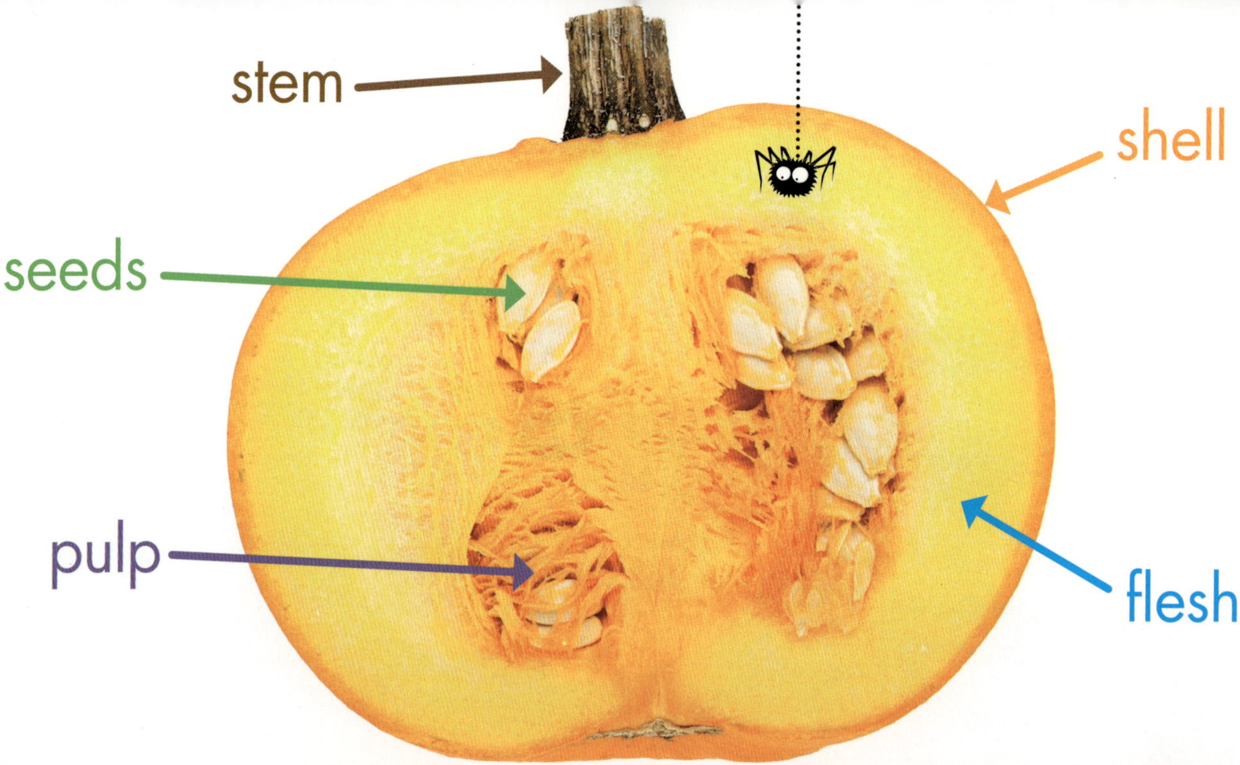

Can you name the parts of this  ?

pumpkin